It's My STATE!

# TEXAS

The Lone Star State

Tatiana Ryckman, Linda Jacobs Altman, Tea Benduhn, and Hex Kleinmartin

Cavendish Square
New York

Published in 2020 by Cavendish Square Publishing, LLC
243 5th Avenue, Suite 136, New York, NY 10016



Fourth Edition



ISBN: 9781502662057

Editorial Director: David McNamara
Editor: Caitlyn Miller
Copy Editor: Nathan Heidelberger
Associate Art Director: Alan Sliwinski
Designer: Jessica Nevins
Production Coordinator: Karol Szymczuk
Photo Research: J8 Media

The photographs in this book are used by permission and through the courtesy of: : Cover f11photo/Shutterstock.com; p. 4 (top, bottom) Cbies/Shutterstock.com, David Lee/Shutterstock.com; p. 5 Kan Khampanya/Shutterstock.com; p. 6 (top, bottom) Svetlana SG/Shutterstock.com, Dennis W Donohue/Shutterstock.com; p. 7 (top, bottom) Ildi Papp/Shutterstock.com, Amar and Isabelle Guillen/Guillen Photo LLC/Alamy Stock Photo; p. 8 Jason Meyer/Alamy Stock Photo; p. 10 (top, bottom) Kisan/Shutterstock.com, Dean Fikar/Shutterstock.com; p. 11 Texas Country/Alamy Stock Photo; p. 12 Album/Alamy Stock Photo; p. 13 Jeffrey M. Frank/Shutterstock.com; p. 14 Hundley Photography/Shutterstock.com; p. 15, 17 Trong Nguyen/Shutterstock.com; p. 16 (top, bottom) f11photo/Shutterstock.com, Roschetzky Photography/Shutterstock.com; p. 18 Rob Nagy/Shutterstock.com; p. 19 (top, bottom) Cire Notrevo/Shutterstock.com, Dean Fikar/Shutterstock.com; p. 20 Johnny Coate/Shutterstock.com; p. 21 Danita Delimont/Gallo Images/Getty Images; p. 22 (top to bottom) G B Hart/Shutterstock.com, By Alissala/Shutterstock.com, Tom Carnes/Shutterstock.com; p. 23 (top to bottom) Milehightraveler/iStock/Getty Images, Steve Bower/Shutterstock.com, Roberto Nistri/Alamy Stock Photo; p. 24 Alfed Eisenstaedt/The LIFE Picture Collection/Getty Images; p. 26 (top, bottom) f11photo/Shutterstock.com, Canadian Copyright Collection held by the British Library/Wikimedia Commons/File:Rene Robert Cavelier de la Salle (HS851016601).Jpg/Public Domain; p. 27 Courtesy Texas Historical Commission; p. 28 APIC/Getty Images; p. 30 Universal History Archive/Getty Images; p. 31 (top, bottom) Bettmann Archive/Getty Images, Everett Historical/Shutterstock.com; p. 32 (top, bottom) Harry Warnecke/NY Daily News Archive/Getty Images, Everett Historical/Shutterstock.com; p. 33 (top to bottom) Photo12/UIG/Getty Images, Keystone/Hulton Archive/Getty Images, Billy Hathorn/Wikimedia Commons/File:Statue of Jose Antonio Navarro, Corsicana, TX IMG0608.JPG/CC BY SA 3.0; p. 35 Pi3.124/Wikimedia Commons/File:Battle of Palmito Ranch Texas historical marker.jpg/Public Domain; p. 36 Buyenlarge/Getty Images; p. 37 Ed Vebell/Getty Images; p. 38 (top, bottom) Loren Elliott/Getty Images, Bettmann/Getty Images; p. 39 Ferd Kaufman/AP Images; p. 40, 41 Bettmann/Getty Images; p. 42 MimaCZ/Shutterstock.com; p. 43 Joe Raedle/Getty Images; p. 44 Kelly/Mooney Photography/Corbis/Getty Images; p. 46 (top, bottom) Paul Komarek/Wikimedia Commons/File:Big Tex 2013.jpg/CC BY SA 3.0, Vinnie Zuffante/Getty Images; p. 47 Natalia Wimberley/Shutterstock.com; p. 48 Lee Russell/Library of Congress/Interim Archives/Getty Images; p. 49 James Southers/Alamy Stock Photo; p. 50 (top, bottom) Kevin Mazur/Getty Images for Parkwood Entertainment/Getty Images, Jesse Grant/Getty Images for WE/Getty Images; p. 51 Gary Miller/Getty Images; p. 52 (top to bottom) Tricia Daniel/Shutterstock.com, Liveon001 ©Travis Witt/Wikimedia Commons/File:Student Center TxState.JPG/CC BY SA 3.0, Denis Tangney Jr/E+/Getty Images; p. 53 Fred LaBounty/Alamy Stock Photo; p. 54 Nancy G Western Photography/Nancy Greifenhagen/Alamy Stock Photo: p. 55 John Moore/Getty Images; p. 58 Shannon Forehand/iStock/Getty Images; p. 60 (top, bottom) Bettmann/Getty Images, Trong Nguyen/Shutterstock.com; p. 61 Asharky/Shutterstock.com; p. 62 Christian Widell/Shutterstock.com; p. 63 Joe Haupt/Wikimedia Commons/File:Vintage Texas Instruments Pocket LCD Calculator, Model TI1750, Made in Japan, Circa 1977(9259570209).jpg/CC BY SA 2.0; p. 64 CJ TravelTips/Wikimedia Commons/File:Schlitterbahn Waterpark Galveston, Texas (5975714079).jpg/CC BY SA 2.0; p. 65 Grexsys/Moment/Getty Images; p. 66 Trong Nguyen/Shutterstock.com; p. 68 RomanSlavik.com/Shutterstock.com; p. 70 (all three), 72 Robert Daemmrich Photography Inc/Corbis/Getty Images; p. 73 Screengrabs; p. 74 Tim Monzingo/The Daily Sentinel/AP Images.

Printed in the United States of America

It's My STATE!

# Table of Contents

# SNAPSHOT OF TEXAS

The Lone Star State

## Statehood

December 29, 1845

## Population

28,304,596
(2017 census estimate)

## Capital

Austin

## State Seal

The Texas state seal has changed five times since it was first introduced, when Texas gained independence from Mexico in 1836. The first government of Texas decided that the original seal would be "a single star of five points, either of gold or silver." In 1839, the seal was updated by state congress to include "an azure ground, encircled by an olive and live oak branches." Though the seal has not changed much since then, it wasn't until 1992 that the seal was standardized to match the exact description in the state constitution. That's more than one hundred years later! Even today, some state offices still use outdated versions of the seal with the wrong kind of oak leaf.

## State Flag

The flag of the Republic of Texas was introduced in 1839. When Texas joined the United States in 1845, that flag was adopted as the state flag. The flag contains three bold stripes of blue, white, and red. The blue stripe is vertical, while the horizontal white stripe is on top of the horizontal red stripe. A single white star is at the center of the blue stripe. The lone star on the flag gave the state its nickname: the Lone Star State. The flag's stripes represent loyalty, bravery, and purity.

## HISTORICAL EVENTS TIMELINE

**1519**
Spanish explorers map the Texas coastline.

**1716–1789**
The Spanish establish missions throughout Texas and the towns of San Antonio, Goliad, and Nacogdoches.

**1821**
Stephen F. Austin founds the first Anglo-American colony in Texas.

## State Song

The Texas state song is "Texas, Our Texas." The song was adopted in 1929 after William J. Marsh and Gladys Yoakum Wright won a statewide contest. The music was originally written by Marsh in 1924. The lyrics say, "Texas, O Texas! your freeborn single star, / Sends out its radiance to nations near and far."

## State Tree

The pecan tree is the state tree of Texas. Fossil records show that pecan trees were living in Texas even before humans. The pecan became the official state tree in 1919 to commemorate James Stephen Hogg, the first native-born governor of Texas. Just before he died in 1906, he asked that a pecan tree be planted at the head of his grave in place of a tombstone. To further prove Texans' love of pecans, the official state health nut is the pecan, and pecan pie is the official state pie.

## State Flower

The bluebonnet is the Texas state flower. These delicate blue flowers bloom along Texas highways, across pastures, and in flowerbeds. However, not all bluebonnets are the same. There are five known varieties across the state, and they are *all* officially the state flower. Any new varieties of bluebonnets that are discovered will also become the state flower.

**1845**

Texas is annexed into the United States.

**1888**

The capitol building in Austin is dedicated.

**1901**

The discovery of **oil** sends Texas into an oil boom.

## State Plant

Prickly Pear Cactus

## State Bird

Mockingbird

**1987**

The first South by Southwest music festival takes place.

**1993**

Kay Bailey Hutchison becomes the first female senator to represent Texas.

**2005**

More than a million Texans evacuate their homes due to Hurricane Rita.

## State Dish

Chili

## State Folk Dance

Square Dance

## CURRENT EVENTS TIMELINE

**2011**

Wildfires destroy more than 1 million acres in Texas.

**2017**

The Houston Astros win the World Series for the first time.

**2018**

Nearly sixteen million Texans register to vote in 2018's midterm elections, a state record.

Guadalupe Peak in West Texas is the highest point in the state.

# 1 Geography

Texas covers 261,232 square miles of the south-central United States. It is the second-largest state in the US. Texas has a diverse landscape, which means there are different types of land throughout the state. There are beaches and marshlands along the Gulf Coast, and cactus grow in the state's desert. Texas is also home to prairies, grasslands, rivers, and forests.

***FAST FACT***

The highest point in Texas is called Guadalupe Peak. It is also known as Signal Peak. This point, located in the Guadalupe Mountains, rises 8,751 feet (2,667 meters) above sea level.

## The Regions of Texas

Texas is made up of 254 counties, the most of any state. Texas is usually divided into four geographic areas: the mountains and basins region in the far west, the Great Plains in the northwest and north-central part of the state, the central lowlands in the middle, and the Gulf Coastal Plain in the east and southeast. These main areas are further divided into smaller areas, or subregions.

### West Texas

The mountains and basins region is also called Big Bend country. A large loop, or bend, in the Rio

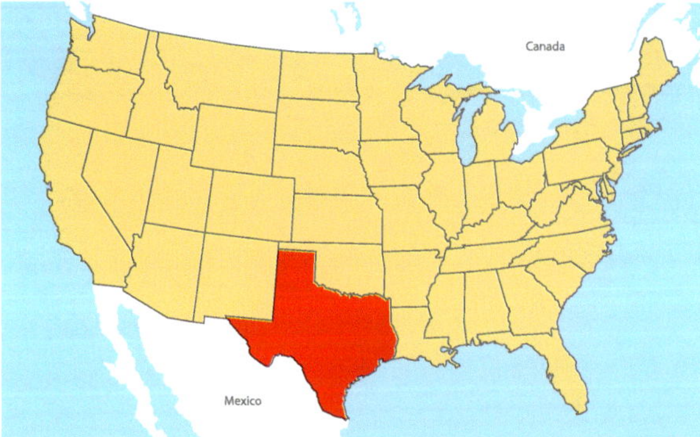


Texas borders the US states of Louisiana, Arkansas, Oklahoma, and New Mexico. Texas also borders the country of Mexico.

Grande ("big river" in Spanish) forms the southern border and separates Texas from Mexico. Big Bend country stretches 41,000 square miles from northeast to southeast.

Big Bend country is made up of basins, or lowlands, and mountain ranges. The area includes the Guadalupe Range, the only true mountains in Texas. The area is also home to Big Bend National Park and Guadalupe Mountains National Park.

Water supply is limited in Big Bend country. The area averages only 13.7 inches of rainfall a year. Due to the lack of water, Big Bend country has very few people. Its only large city is El Paso, which had an estimated **population** of 683,577 in 2017.

The high plains region of the Texas Panhandle lies to the northeast of Big Bend country. This dry plateau (raised flat land) is split in the north by the Canadian River. The weather is very different across the region. The prairie is very windy, and there are often flash

Big Bend National Park is a popular destination for hikers and nature lovers.

floods. Storms called "blue northers" bring freezing winds from the Rocky Mountains.

The Panhandle is cattle country. Herds of beef cattle graze here. Though the region is about the size of West Virginia, its total population is only about 500,000. About 454,000 of those residents live in the two biggest cities, Amarillo and Lubbock. The rest are spread among ranches and country towns so small that they don't have a grocery store.

## Central Texas

The Caprock Escarpment is a steep cliff on the eastern edge of the Panhandle plateau. It separates the high plains of the Panhandle from the lower central plains. This area was once a prairie where huge herds of bison lived. Today, the bison are gone, and so is the tall grass. The region is the most populated in Texas, with most people clustered in the Dallas–Fort Worth area.

South of the rolling plains is the Edwards Plateau, or hill country. The ground is rougher but not very high. The area is dotted with rivers, streams, and lakes. It is known for its beauty and is considered the heart of Texas.

An area called the Balcones Canyonlands is northwest of Austin. It has ancient rock formations and cliff faces so steep they seem like walls.

## East Texas

The coastal plain of East Texas is the largest natural region in the state. The northwestern part of the area has many

### FAST FACT

The Tyler Municipal Rose Garden, roughly 100 miles (161 km) from Dallas, is the largest rose garden in the United States. This 14-acre (6 ha) garden showcases six hundred varieties of roses and more than thirty-eight thousand rose bushes.

Rock formations in Balcones Canyonlands are named for their unique look. The Spanish explorer Bernardo de Miranda y Flores thought the rocks resembled balconies sticking out of the hills.

# A Changing Map of Texas

Alonso Álvarez de Pineda, a Spanish explorer, was the first European to sketch the Texas coastline. Pineda drew the first physical map of Texas, but it is Álvar Núñez Cabeza de Vaca who is known for first capturing life in Texas with his writing. In *The Account*, the book about his travels from Florida to Mexico, he tells tales of Native Americans, terrible misfortunes, and great adventure.

Cabeza de Vaca wrote of his struggles in crossing Texas in the year 1527:

> Indians guided us through more than fifty leagues of deserted land in very rugged sierras … At the end [we crossed] a great river in which the water came up to our chests. And thus we … traversed the entire land until coming out at the South Sea. [We] walked another seventeen days in the direction of the sunset … and there we found people who eat nothing but powders of grass for a third of the year.

Álvar Núñez Cabeza de Vaca explored Texas and wrote a book about his adventures there.

For hundreds of years after Cabeza de Vaca's visit to Texas, there was no border between Texas and Mexico. The entire area was controlled by Spain. Though Texas gained independence in 1836, it wasn't until the end of the Mexican-American War in 1848 that the Rio Grande was set as the border between Mexico and the United States.

Though the Treaty of Guadalupe Hidalgo was thought to have made the boundary between Mexico and Texas clear, a large flood in the 1860s caused the Rio Grande to shift. This shift moved roughly 600 acres (243 hectares) of land from Mexico to the United States. This land was

The Chamizal National Memorial in El Paso celebrates the end of a land dispute between Mexico and the United States.

referred to as Chamizal and was fought over for nearly one hundred years. In 1964, President John F. Kennedy came to an agreement with the Mexican government, returning 366 acres of land to Mexico.

Texas has also fought with US states over its borders. The eastern border with Louisiana was renegotiated as recently as the 1970s. Texas's northern border with Oklahoma has been debated for the last two hundred years. As recently as 2013, Texas lawmakers were looking into redrawing that state line.

The Gulf Coast of Texas

oak trees and other hardwoods. These forests alternate with blackland prairies, where the soil is dark and rich.

To the east, along the Louisiana border, are pine trees that once covered much of the southeast. The largest city in the region is Tyler, with about 105,000 people.

The Texas coastline is on the Gulf of Mexico. The Gulf Coast is a place of sandy beaches and wetlands, or marshes. The Gulf Coast is filled with wildlife, including whooping cranes and sea turtles.

Inland from the Gulf is the Rio Grande Valley—the southernmost tip of the Gulf Coastal Plain. The valley is a lowland desert, with mesquite trees, prickly pear cactus, and rootless tumbleweeds blowing in the wind. **Irrigation** systems bring in water to help make the soil fertile for crops. Farms there produce a variety of fruits and vegetables, including spinach, peanuts, and strawberries.

Texas has several barrier islands that extend along the Gulf Coast. These landforms include Galveston Island and Padre Island. Padre

### FAST FACT

The first suspension bridge ever built in Texas was constructed across the Brazos River in Waco. Built in 1870, the Waco bridge spans 475 feet (145 m) and contains nearly three million bricks. At the time, this was the only way to safely cross the Brazos, and the price tag of $140,000 was quickly earned back in tolls.

# Visiting the Alamo

The Alamo is one of the most iconic—and most visited—historic landmarks in Texas. In 2015, the site hosted more than one million visitors. The building is a Franciscan mission, built by a group of early Spanish **settlers**. The mission served its intended purpose as a church from roughly 1718 until the late 1700s. That's when Spanish authorities gave the land of five missions in the area to residents. In late 1835, the Alamo was taken over by Texas forces demanding independence from Mexico. Mexican forces returned to reclaim the Alamo in February 1836.

To many Texans, the Alamo is a symbol of strength and independence, no matter the odds. The small group of Texan soldiers who fought at the Alamo stood almost no chance of winning the battle (they were outnumbered roughly seven to one). Still, they felt it was important to fight for independence. The Texans lost that battle, but they provided a memorable slogan: "Remember the Alamo!" Ten years later, this famous saying was used during the Mexican-American War.

Though the building itself is still a modest, one-room mission, visitors flock to the historic site. The Alamo helps Texans connect with their patriotic history.

The Alamo is one of the most famous landmarks in Texas.

# Texas' Biggest Cities

*(Population numbers are from the US Census Bureau's 2017 projections for incorporated cities.)*

Houston

Austin

## 1. Houston: population 2,312,717

Houston is the most populous city in Texas and the fourth most populous city in the United States. It was incorporated as a city in 1837. Houston's economy is diverse—the city's big industries include transportation and **manufacturing**.

## 2. San Antonio: population 1,511,946

San Antonio, officially the City of San Antonio, was first founded by the Spanish in 1718. The people of San Antonio work in fields like health care, tourism, and oil and gas.

## 3. Dallas: population 1,341,075

Dallas was important in American history thanks to its oil production. Dallas was founded in 1841 and formally incorporated in February 1856. Today, it is known as a major center for business and culture.

## 4. Austin: population 950,715

Austin was selected as the site of the Texas capital in 1839. Residents and visitors enjoy the arts, music, and food scenes the city offers. Austin has become famous around the world for its festivals.

## 5. Fort Worth: population 874,168

Fort Worth was founded in 1849. The city is home to Texas Christian University, Texas Wesleyan University, the University of North Texas Health Science Center, and Texas A&M University School of Law.

## 6. El Paso: population 683,577

El Paso was incorporated in 1873, though the Spanish had first settled there between 1681 and 1682. The city is across the border from Juárez, Chihuahua, Mexico. Workers from Juárez cross into El Paso every day, and workers from El Paso cross into Juárez to go to their jobs too.

## 7. Arlington: population 396,394

Arlington was named for General Robert E. Lee's Arlington House in Virginia. The city incorporated in 1884. Today, the Dallas Cowboys are based in Arlington and play at AT&T Stadium.

## 8. Corpus Christi: population 325,605

Corpus Christi incorporated in 1852. The city is nicknamed "Texas Riviera" and "Sparkling City by the Sea" because of its location on the coast. Corpus Christi is home to one of the largest ports in the country.

Corpus Christi

## 9. Plano: population 286,143

Plano has been designated the best place to live in the western United States and the eleventh best place to live in the United States by *Money* magazine. It also has been named as the safest city in America by *Forbes*.

## 10. Laredo: population 260,654

Founded in 1755, Laredo boasts the largest inland port on the US-Mexico border. More than 47 percent of United States trade to Mexico and more than 36 percent of Mexican trade to the United States crosses through Laredo.

Island is the longest barrier island in the world. Barrier islands are offshore islands that protect mainlands from storms. The Gulf Coast is often hit by hurricanes and other tropical storms.

## Climate

Texans have been known to say that their state has four seasons: drought, flood, blizzard, and twister (tornado). Like many jokes, this one has a bit of truth. All these extremes can and do happen in Texas's **climate**.

West Texas is the coldest part of the state, with an average annual temperature of 54 degrees Fahrenheit. Summer days are fiercely hot, but temperatures get much colder at night. Even in July and August, West Texans often need a sweater after sunset. Winter brings blizzards that blanket the prairie in snow.

The hottest part of Texas is the Rio Grande Valley, known for mild winters and hot summers. On the Gulf Coast, the marine air from the Gulf of Mexico means it is not as hot. But the humidity is still high. Winters are equally mild, with no snow. But this mild weather can be spoiled by fierce, often deadly storms coming from the Gulf.

In the northern prairie regions of Texas, it's not uncommon to see snow.

## Wildlife

Like the climate and the land, Texas wildlife varies by region. It ranges from rattlesnakes and roadrunners in the western desert to beavers, raccoons, and white-tailed deer in the eastern woodlands.

Hurricane Harvey batters Kemah in 2017.

Majestic whooping cranes spend their winters on the Gulf Coast, and sea turtles swim just offshore. Alligators prowl the marshlands, occasionally coming into contact with human beings. Game wardens at the Texas Parks and Wildlife Department receive hundreds of "nuisance alligator" calls each year.

The Rio Grande Valley has some of the state's most unusual animal species. Tropical creatures such as the ocelot and the coatimundi have migrated north from Mexico. The coatimundi, or coati for short, is related to the raccoon. It looks a bit like a raccoon but has a longer face and tail. It looks for food in trees as well as on the ground, living mainly on insects.

Texas is home to more than one hundred species and subspecies of snakes, including the rattlesnake.

Coatimundis make a home in Texas.

## Endangered Species

The Kemp's ridley is the smallest and most endangered kind of sea turtle in the world. They have an average length of 23 to 27.5 inches and average weight of 100 pounds. The turtles' nesting areas are found only in Mexico and Texas. In 1985, there were only 702 nests for these turtles worldwide, the lowest total ever. Scientists have been working to help the species make a comeback.

Biologists now watch for new turtle nests. Then, they place the eggs in an incubator for protected care. After the eggs hatch, many of the babies are "head-started." This means that hatchlings grow in captivity. When the turtles are big enough, volunteers release them into the Gulf of Mexico. Protecting the eggs and hatchlings has helped stop the Kemp's ridley population from dying out. The population has increased to about twelve thousand.

The ocelot is a cat about twice the size of an ordinary house cat. It lives in southern Texas, hunting birds, rabbits, and small rodents. The most striking feature of the ocelot is its beautiful spotted fur. For many years, its fur made the cat a favorite target for hunters. The ocelot lives in

Ocelots live in the southern regions of Texas. Because of their unique fur, ocelots were popular game for hunters before being added to the endangered species list.

dense brush, and much of its habitat has been cut down for farmland. Today, the ocelot is on the US government's endangered species list.

Texas has experienced a large population boom in recent years, and the state's towns and cities continue to grow. Population growth can be hard on wild animals and natural habitats. Luckily, the people of Texas want to make sure there are still open spaces in their state. Many organizations have been formed to help protect wildlife, endangered species, and the rich natural landscape in this time of change.

# What Lives in Texas?

Agave

Indian paintbrush

Yucca

## Flora

**Agave** Agave is a beautiful blue-gray plant that regularly grows to 6 feet (1.8 m) tall. This spiny plant lives for ten to twenty years before sending up a massive, 15-foot (4.6 m) flowering stalk.

**Cactus** There are more than one hundred species of cactus in Texas, a greater variety than is found in any other state. Most of these varieties are found in West Texas, near Big Bend.

**Indian Paintbrush** Castilleja, or Indian paintbrush, is a common sight along Texas roadways. These vibrant coral wildflowers dot the landscape in natural places but are hard to grow in gardens.

**Mesquite** Mesquite trees grow across Texas. Ranchers struggle with the thorny trees because they can injure cattle. However, the mesquite is impressive for its long taproot—some can be up to 175 feet (53 m) long—which helps it access scarce water.

**Yuccas** There are roughly twenty species of yucca that grow across Texas. These squat, spiny trees produce an edible flowering stalk. Historically, the fibers of the tough leaves were soaked and then twisted into cord. Yucca roots contain saponin, a chemical that can be used as a natural soap.

## Fauna

**Mexican Free-Tailed Bat** The Mexican free-tailed bat is the most common bat found in Texas, but they don't live there year-round. They live in caves in Mexico throughout the winter and begin their migration north in February. These bats can fly up to 60 miles per hour (97 kilometers per hour) and often fly 100 miles (161 km) in an evening while looking for food.

Mexican free-tailed bat

**Nine-Banded Armadillo** This cat-sized, armored animal is famous for digging for both food and shelter. Babies are always born in sets of four, and armadillos are the only mammal to have multiple offspring from each of their eggs. Though long associated with Texas, armadillos are originally from South America and can be found as far north as Kansas.

Nine-banded armadillo

**Texas Blind Salamander** The Texas blind salamander is an endangered species, living primarily in the Edwards Aquifer in San Marcos, Texas. Because they live underground, these salamanders have no eyes. This thin, white creature hunts for food by sensing the movement of the water.

**Texas Map Turtle** This species of turtle, popular among pet-owners, is found where the Colorado River drains into the Edwards Plateau. The Texas map turtle gets its name from the yellow and red lines on its carapace, or shell, which resemble a road map.

Texas map turtle

**White-Tailed Deer** Texas is home to roughly 3.6 million white-tailed deer. These deer use the white bottom of their tails to warn others of danger. Their diet is usually made up of weeds and occasionally woody plants and bark.

Cowboys and ranchers have long been associated with the wide-open spaces of Texas.

# 2 The History of Texas

Texas has a rich, multicultural history. Long before **cowboys** herded cattle, **Native Americans** lived in different parts of the state. The Caddo lived in the east. The Atakapa and Karankawa lived on the coast. The Tonkawa and Tigua lived in the west. When European settlers came to the area, they began fighting over the land. By 1845, Texas had been controlled by five different countries.

Texas was claimed for Spain by the first explorers of the area. Later, the territory was claimed by France, then Mexico, and for a short time it existed as the independent Texas Republic. In 1845, Texas joined the United States, but things still weren't settled. During the Civil War, Texas was considered part of the Confederacy. Once the Civil War was over, Texas rejoined the United States.

**FAST FACT**

In 1839, the town of Waterloo became the capital of Texas and was renamed Austin after Stephen F. Austin. In 1842, under threat of attack from Mexico, the capital was moved back to Houston for two years before returning to Austin for good.

The first Spanish settlements were built around missions, like this one in San Antonio.

## Spanish Texas

Spanish interest in Texas began as early as 1519, when a sea captain named Alonso Álvarez de Pineda mapped the Gulf coastline.

Between 1681 and 1682, the first permanent European settlement in present-day Texas was built near the modern city of El Paso. As the Spanish claimed and settled lands, they had problems with the people who already lived there. The Europeans forced the Native Americans off of their land. As a result, the Native Americans lost their way of life.

Some Native American groups were conquered. After members converted to Christianity, they were made to work for the Spanish missions. The missions were not just churches. They were complete settlements that also included workshops, supply rooms, and living quarters. The Native Americans who were forced to convert lived at the mission and worked long, hard hours in the fields. They did not get paid for this work, nor were they allowed to leave.

Many of the Native people got sick from European diseases such as smallpox and measles. Native Americans had not experienced these illnesses. Theys had no resistance, or immunity, to them. Many groups were wiped out by diseases.

The Native Americans that did survive lived by raiding Spanish settlements. For as long as the Spanish flag flew over Texas, settlers were locked in a bloody struggle with the Native people.

La Salle, a French explorer, arrived in Texas by mistake.

## French Settlers

In 1684, King Louis XIV of France gave the explorer René-Robert Cavelier, sieur de La Salle, four ships. The king commanded La Salle to set up a fort at the mouth of the Mississippi River in what is now Louisiana. But La Salle made a mistake when he was navigating his ships. He landed in East Texas instead of Louisiana.

La Salle decided to make the best of the situation and built the fort in Texas. The result was Fort St. Louis, named in honor of the king.

The explorer soon realized that he had chosen a bad location. Fort St. Louis was built on marshland in the heart of Karankawa territory. The Karankawas captured or killed many of the French. In 1687, La Salle was killed when his men staged a mutiny (a revolt against a person in charge). Sometime later, Karankawa warriors overran the fort.

Fort St. Louis

Other Frenchmen continued to settle on the Gulf Coast of Louisiana and Texas until 1763, when France lost most of its American land to Great Britain and Spain. The British claimed France's territory east of the Mississippi River, while Spain took the territory west of the Mississippi River. Spain later returned the Louisiana Territory to France, which then sold it to the United States in in the 1803 Louisiana Purchase.

## Mexican Settlers and the War for Independence

In 1821, Mexico won its independence from Spain. A new flag flew over Texas: the eagle banner of the Mexican nation. The new Mexican government was not very interested in Texas. An American named Stephen F. Austin was, however. With the permission of the Mexican government, he started an American colony in northeastern Texas. In return for land, he agreed that the settlers would become citizens of Mexico and obey its laws. Austin himself kept this agreement, but it was harder to control the settlers.

# The Native People of Texas

Traditional native groups that lived in Texas included the Apache, Atakapa, Bidai, Caddo, Coahuiltecan, Comanche, Hasinai, Jumano, Karankawa, and Tonkawa, though the Comanche were latecomers. They arrived in the area just before the Europeans did. During the early 1800s, however, many more Native Americans moved into Texas. This is because many Native Americans had been pushed out of their traditional lands to the east by American settlement and expansion. These nations included the Cherokee, Choctaw, Chickasaw, Kickapoo, and Shawnee.

In the 1800s, Native Americans who had been pushed off their land in other states made their way to Texas.

The original Native Americans of Texas had been living in the area for more than ten thousand years. Some were hunters and gatherers, and others were farming people. In Texas's many regions, Native American groups lived in many different types of houses. Some could be set up quickly and were portable, which made them well suited to a nomadic lifestyle, like the tepee (a conical tent of poles and animal skins). Others were permanent dwellings for farming people who couldn't leave their fields or harvests, like the stone and adobe buildings known as pueblos.

Only three recognized nations remain in Texas. The others were killed or forced to disband or relocate. Some of these, like the Comanche, fought back against the Europeans, while some disbanded and integrated into Texan society.

## Spotlight on the Caddo

The name Caddo comes from their own name for themselves, Kadohadacho. The original meaning of that name isn't known for certain. Some Caddo people think it comes from the phrase "true chiefs." Caddo words are important in Texas. The name Texas (or Tejas) comes from a Caddo word that means "friends" or "allies."

**Region:** Historically, the Caddo lived in Texas, Oklahoma, Arkansas, and Louisiana. Most Caddo people today live in Oklahoma.

**Homes:** The Caddo in Texas built pole and earthen lodges with roofs of thatched grass. Many Caddo villages were circled by protective walls.

**Food:** The Caddo farmed beans, pumpkins, sunflowers, and corn. Caddo women were in charge of the harvest. Caddo men were hunters and fishermen. Soup was a common Caddo dish, as was cornbread.

**Clothing:** The Caddo wore clothes made from woven cloth and animal hides. Women wore skirts, while men wore leggings. Men and women wore moccasins.

The Texas War for Independence began in 1835 due to frustrations between the Mexican government and the new American settlers.

Many settlers were Mexican citizens in name only. They did not understand the culture or the language. Some settlers from the United States brought enslaved people to Texas, even though slavery was illegal under Mexican law. It was only a matter of time before disagreements between these two very different cultures turned into a war.

That war began in October 1835, when a group of Texans defeated a Mexican force trying to capture the Texans at the town of Gonzales, near San Antonio. On March 2, 1836, Texas declared independence from Mexico. Texan leaders met at Washington-on-the-Brazos. Meanwhile, Mexican troops were attacking the Alamo in San Antonio, which had been captured by Texan forces in December 1835. For thirteen days, a force of 190 to 260 Texans held off an army of nearly 2,000 Mexican soldiers. Though all the Texans were killed when Mexican troops launched a full-scale attack on March 6, their bravery gave hope to the Texan forces.

On April 21, 1836, Sam Houston led an army of Texans against Mexican forces at San Jacinto. Houston knew how to plan a battle. He was able to inspire his soldiers to defeat a much larger force of professional soldiers. The battle lasted

### FAST FACT

Sam Houston was actually born in Virginia. He ran away to Tennessee as a child and eventually became governor there. Later, after serving as the president of Texas, Houston was elected governor of Texas. He is the only person to have been elected governor of two different states.

only eighteen minutes, and Houston's army won the day. The land they fought on is near what is now the city of Houston. Antonio López de Santa Anna, the Mexican leader, was captured after the battle. He agreed that Texas could have its independence. Sam Houston became a Texas hero.

The now-famous Lone Star banner of Texas became the flag of the new state. Sam Houston became its first president, and Stephen F. Austin was named its secretary of state.

Texas Rangers in the late 1800s

## Statehood and the Mexican-American War

Stephen F. Austin first brought together a group of volunteers, whom he called Rangers, to patrol and protect settlers. The Texas Rangers became an officially recognized special police force in 1835. These men were in charge of protecting settlers against bandits and Native American raids. Texas still faced threats from Mexico and Native Americans. Many Texans believed the only way to be truly protected was to become a part of the United States.

James Polk was president during the Mexican-American War.

In order to become a state, Texas needed to form a stable government. There was another issue: slavery was legal in Texas. Some US states that had abolished, or ended, slavery did not want to allow Texas to become a state. Nevertheless, in 1845, the US Congress voted to admit Texas to the Union (the United States). It became the twenty-eighth state.

When Texas became a state, US president James Polk wanted its southern border to be the Rio Grande river. Mexico disagreed with the location of the border. Polk offered to buy Mexican land in the region, but Mexico refused to sell. It also renounced, or took back, its recognition of Texas

### FAST FACT

While some people claim that Texas can **secede** from the Union at any time, that's not really true. What is true is that Texas can be broken up into as many as five US states.

# Texas's Important People

Dwight D. Eisenhower

Sam Houston

## Stephen F. Austin

Stephen Fuller Austin is considered the "Father of Texas." Born in Virginia in 1793, Austin famously founded the first successful Anglo-American settlement in the Texas territory. Today, the state capital is named in his honor, as well as a county and two colleges.

## Dwight D. Eisenhower

Dwight D. Eisenhower was born in Denison, Texas. He became the thirty-fourth president of the United States. Before becoming president, he served in the US Army. As a general, Eisenhower was the supreme commander of Allied forces for Western Europe during World War II.

## Miriam Amanda Wallace Ferguson

Miriam Ferguson was the first female governor of Texas. She was first elected in 1924, only four years after women were given the right to vote. Ferguson won a second term in 1932. She opposed the Ku Klux Klan and prohibition (a legal ban on selling alcohol), which were the major issues of her day.

## Matt Gaines

Matt Gaines was born into slavery in Louisiana. He escaped slavery twice but was caught both times. After he gained free status, Gaines became a leading member of the black community in Texas as a preacher and a politician. In 1870, he was elected to the Texas state senate. Gaines advocated for education for emancipated slaves, prison reform, and protection at the **polls**.

## Sam Houston

Sam Houston led the battle that won Texas's independence from Mexico. He became the first president of the Republic of Texas. Houston worked to make Texas part of the United States. When this was achieved in 1845, he became a US senator.

## Lyndon B. Johnson

Lyndon B. Johnson was born in Stonewall, Texas, in 1908. In 1963, he became the thirty-sixth president of the United States. Johnson had been John F. Kennedy's vice president. When Kennedy was killed, he took over the presidency. In the following election, Johnson won by a landslide. As president, he focused on reducing poverty and improving civil rights.

Lyndon B. Johnson

## Anson Jones

Anson Jones was the fourth and final president of the Republic of Texas. Though he began his professional life as a schoolteacher and a physician in the Northeast, he made his way south. Jones then began a political career. He worked with Sam Houston to make Texas attractive to the United States so that Texas could become a state.

## Barbara Jordan

Barbara Jordan

In 1966, Barbara Jordan became the first African American woman elected to the Texas state senate. Six years later, she became the first African American woman from the South elected to the US House of Representatives. Jordan worked to protect people of color and the poor. She received many awards, including the Spingarn Medal from the NAACP and the Presidential Medal of Freedom.

## José Antonio Navarro

José Antonio Navarro was part of a noble family and a resident of San Antonio. Navarro was a Tejano, or a Mexican American living in Texas, who advocated for Texas's separation from Mexico. He developed a friendship with Stephen F. Austin and helped him get the proper documents to bring settlers to the area. After Texas won its independence from Mexico, Navarro fought for legal citizenship for Tejanos.

José Antonio Navarro

independence. Polk responded by sending American troops to Texas in 1846.

When US troops moved into the land Mexico claimed as theirs, Mexican soldiers shot at them. General Zachary Taylor sent word to President Polk that fighting had begun. The United States officially declared war on Mexico on May 13. The war ended with an American victory almost two years after it began.

The United States and Mexico signed the Treaty of Guadalupe Hidalgo on February 2, 1848. Mexico was forced to give up its claim to Texas. It also gave up territory that included what is now California, Nevada, and Utah, as well as parts of Arizona, New Mexico, Colorado, and Wyoming. In return, the United States gave Mexico $15 million (about $480 million in today's money).

The end of the war did not stop border fights in the Rio Grande Valley or Native American raids in the west. South and West Texas remained dangerous places for settlers. East Texas, however, was not as violent. It became a vast cotton-growing area, with much of the land owned by white "gentlemen farmers" and worked by enslaved African Americans.

## The Civil War

In November 1860, Abraham Lincoln was elected president of the United States. Although he disagreed with slavery, he had said he would not end it in the states where it already existed. Still, many people in the South did not want to remain part of the United States. Between December 1860 and the spring of 1861, eleven Southern states, including Texas, seceded (withdrew) from the Union and joined together as the Confederate States of America. The sixth flag of Texas was the Confederate flag.

Not many battles were fought on Texas soil during the Civil War, but the state contributed sixty thousand soldiers, plus large amounts of ammunition and other supplies, to the Confederate army.

The Civil War officially ended in a Union victory when Confederate general Robert E. Lee surrendered to Union general Ulysses S. Grant on April 9, 1865. However, the last battle of the war, the Battle of Palmito Ranch, was fought in the Lone Star State near Brownsville more than a month later.

For the second half of the 1860s, Texas was under the control of a US military government. In order to rejoin the Union, Texas had to do several things. It had to pass a new state constitution. It also had to ratify (approve) three new amendments to the US Constitution. The Thirteenth Amendment abolished slavery. The Fourteenth Amendment guaranteed all people equal protection under the law. The Fifteenth Amendment granted African American men the right to vote. After meeting all these requirements, Texas was allowed to rejoin the Union in 1870.

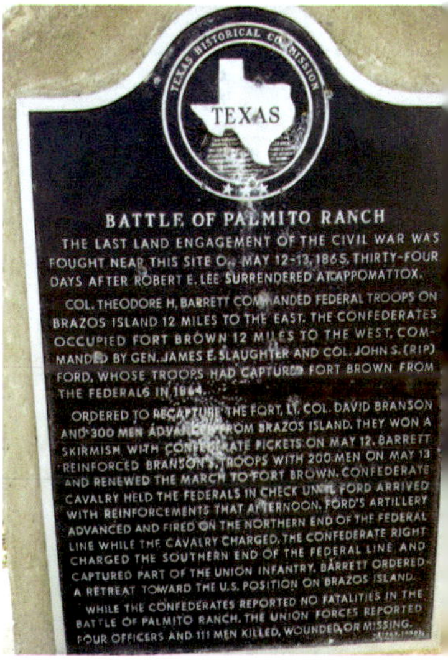


The Battle of Palmito Ranch—the last battle of the Civil War—was fought a month after the war officially ended.

## The Golden Age of Cowboys

In the second half of the 1800s, cattle raising became more important in West Texas, where there was enough grazing land to support large herds. Before railroads reached many parts of Texas in the 1880s, ranchers and the cowboys who worked for them organized huge annual cattle drives to take the cattle to market. The men and hundreds of thousands of cattle often covered distances of up to 1,000 miles to reach railroad lines in Kansas or Missouri.

# Juneteenth: A Texas Holiday

On June 19, 1865, Union soldiers arrived in Galveston, Texas. They were there to announce the emancipation, or freeing, of enslaved people throughout the South. This news arrived two and a half years after President Abraham Lincoln's Emancipation Proclamation in January of 1863. (Lincoln's proclamation had officially granted free status to any enslaved people in the Confederacy.) Major General Gordon Granger, who led the Union troops, read the following declaration in Galveston:

> The people of Texas are informed that, in accordance with a Proclamation from the Executive of the United States, all slaves are free. This involves an absolute equality of personal rights and rights of property between former masters and slaves, and the connection heretofore existing between them becomes that between employer and hired labor.

Juneteenth celebrates the emancipation of enslaved African Americans after the Civil War. Here, Bill and Ellen Thomas, formerly enslaved people, are photographed in Hondo, Texas, in 1937.

Juneteenth is an annual celebration of this late-arriving news for enslaved people in Texas. African Americans who now had free status came together around food and talked about a shared commitment to self-improvement and societal change.

In the early 1900s, as black and white societies began merging, celebrations focusing on black history were stifled. People stopped celebrating Juneteenth. In the 1950s and 1960s, however, the civil rights movement brought new interest in the history and traditions of African Americans. In 1979, Texas made Juneteenth (June 19) an official state holiday, and many other states have made it a holiday since then.

A crew of twelve men could drive a herd of three thousand cattle. While herds were made up of livestock from several owners, all of the animals were branded with the same road brand. The drive could cover 10 to 15 miles per day, so a drive to Kansas could take one hundred days.

The slow-moving herds were often easy prey for outlaws, such as **cattle rustlers** (thieves). These outlaws were usually cowboys who knew how to ride horses and rope cattle and were familiar with the countryside. The Texas Rangers, legendary for their horsemanship and their marksmanship, were the main defenders of law and order in many areas. In Texas at this time, if a person was caught rustling cattle, he might be hanged.

Though it is an important part of Texas history, the age of the cattle drives lasted only about twenty years. Cattle drives became unnecessary once railroads and refrigeration came to the region in the 1880s.

A typical cattle drive from Texas to Kansas could take about one hundred days.

## Texas in the Twentieth Century

Texas began the 1900s with a major discovery. In 1901, mining engineer A. F. Lucas struck oil at Spindletop. When the "gusher" shot into the air, it changed American industry. According to geologist Michael T. Halbouty, Spindletop "started the liquid fuel age, which brought forth the automobile, the airplane, the network of highways … [and] untold comforts and conveniences."

When the United States entered World War I in 1917, the army found that the wide-open spaces of Texas were ideal locations for training bases. Soldiers from all over the country went to Texas. Kelly Field in San Antonio was the first base for training pilots to fly the new airplanes that would

The first National Aeronautics and Space Administration (NASA) space center is in Houston.

be dogfighting in the skies of Europe. (A dogfight is an air battle between planes.)

By 1961, people were ready to fly even farther. The National Aeronautics and Space Administration (NASA) opened a space center in Houston. There, NASA scientists and engineers designed and developed the spacecraft and managed the missions that took American astronauts into space. In 1969, ground controllers in Houston worked with astronauts aboard the *Apollo 11* spacecraft. These men became the first humans to land and walk on the moon.

## Texas Becomes More Urban

After World War II (1939–1945), education became important for many Americans returning from the war. Texas A&M and the University of Texas became nationally important. Many veterans enrolled in college after the war.

In the 1950s, a severe drought caused many ranchers and farmers to find new ways to make money. Many people moved from farmland (rural areas) into the cities (urban areas). The cities grew, and the rural areas shrank.

Many changes needed to take place for Texas's cities to support bigger populations. The larger cities needed much more water, so the state formed the Texas Water Development Board. The Austin Area Economic Foundation worked to get more technology manufacturers into the capital city of Austin.

The University of Texas became well-known as a research facility after World War II.

## Civil Rights

Just like other states, Texas had segregation (separation of black and white people). In the late 1800s and early 1900s, laws kept African Americans from going to the same schools and using the same public facilities as white people. Ethel Minor of the National Association for the Advancement of Colored People (NAACP) recalled, "'Colored only' signs were everywhere. There were a lot of places where we weren't allowed to try on clothes."

The civil rights movement was a nationwide movement begun in the 1950s to gain equal rights for African Americans. It included marches and demonstrations, public protests, and court cases to overturn segregation laws. One important Texas case in 1950 allowed an African American student to attend the University of Texas Law School. This happened four years before the historic US Supreme Court decision that outlawed racial segregation in schools all over the country.

The struggle for equal rights continued through the 1900s and came to include Mexican Americans and other groups besides African Americans. Activist Thomas C. Rockeymoore of the Texas NAACP spoke of the importance of ending inequality when he said, "Discrimination affects all of us, no matter what race you happen to be."

Texas played a large role in the passing of the Civil Rights Act in 1964. However, its part came about because of one of the saddest incidents in the history

Protesters march in Dallas in 1964 to demand desegregation of schools.

of the state and of the nation—the assassination of John F. Kennedy.

## Johnson and Kennedy

Lyndon Baines Johnson was born in Stonewall, Texas, in 1908 and was elected to the United States Senate in 1948. In 1953, he became the youngest minority leader (the head of the party with fewer senators) in US Senate history. When the Democrats gained control of the Senate in 1954, he became the majority leader.

Johnson ran for president in 1960 but lost the Democratic nomination to John F. Kennedy, a war hero from Massachusetts. Johnson had strong support in the South, so Kennedy selected him as his vice presidential running mate. Together, they won the election.

On November 22, 1963, President Kennedy was riding in a motorcade through Dallas when he was killed by a sniper's bullet. Texas governor John Connally was also injured in the car, but he recovered completely from his wounds. Vice President Johnson, who had been riding in a vehicle two cars behind Kennedy, was sworn in as the thirty-sixth president of the United States aboard *Air Force One*, the president's airplane, as it flew back to Washington, DC.

President John F. Kennedy was assassinated on November 22, 1963, in Dallas.

As vice president, Johnson had worked closely with President Kennedy on equal rights for minorities. Continuing this important goal, President Johnson pushed a civil rights bill proposed by Kennedy through Congress before the next election. Key points in this bill included:

- Outlawing discrimination in theaters, motels, restaurants, and other public places
- Outlawing different voting rules for people of different races and economic status
- Desegregation of public schools

- Outlawing discrimination in employment and establishment of the Equal Employment Opportunity Commission

In 1964, Lyndon B. Johnson signed an important equal rights bill into law.

Before he signed the bill on July 2, 1964, Johnson said:

> We believe that all men are created equal—yet many are denied equal treatment. We believe that all men have certain **unalienable rights**—yet many Americans do not enjoy those rights. We believe that all men are entitled to the blessings of liberty—yet millions are being deprived of those blessings, not because of their own failures, but because of the color of their skins.

Johnson was elected to his own presidential term in 1964 but was faced with many problems in addition to racial discrimination. The biggest problem was the Vietnam War, which the US became more involved in after Johnson was elected president. However, he was able to establish two federal programs that continue to help a lot of people: Medicare and Medicaid.

## Growth, Change, and Recovery

At the end of the 1900s, the economy of Texas grew. Texans worked hard to enter new industries. In 2008, that hard work paid off when the US economy entered a recession. A recession is when the economy shrinks. Because Texas had so many opportunities for its residents, the Lone Star State was not hit as hard by the recession as other states were. Texas recovered quickly.

# Make Your Own Pinwheel

Texas leads the nation in wind-powered energy. Since 2014, wind turbines in Texas have produced more electricity than both of the state's nuclear power plants. You can build your own miniature wind turbine with this simple pinwheel tutorial.

## Supplies:

- 1 4-inch (10 cm) square piece of heavy cardstock
- Ruler
- Pencil with eraser attached
- Scissors
- Stapler or glue
- Straight pin

## Directions:

1. Use your ruler to draw straight lines diagonally across the cardstock from one corner to the other, making an X across the square.
2. Cut along these lines until you're ¾ inch (2 cm) from the center of the square. This will make four triangles, connected at the center of the paper.
3. Fold the left corner of each triangle toward the center, stapling or gluing them all in place. You should now have the head of the pinwheel.
4. Make a stem for the pinwheel by pushing a straight pin through the center of the pinwheel, and into the eraser of the pencil.
5. Blow on your new pinwheel or place it in front of a fan to see it in action!

However, Texas has had some hard times in recent years. In 2008, Hurricane Ike was responsible for the deaths of more than eighty Texans. The hurricane caused $34.8 billion of damage, particularly in the Bolivar Peninsula, Houston, and Galveston. Texans had to face another deadly hurricane in 2017, when Hurricane Harvey made landfall between Port O'Connor and Port Aransas. That storm was responsible for $125 billion in damage and killed almost ninety people.

Because of the damage caused by Hurricane Ike and Hurricane Harvey, the World Meteorological Society (WMS) has retired the names "Ike" and "Harvey" for Atlantic hurricanes. (The WMS chooses names for storms and usually repeats names over time.)

Communities pulled together to rebuild after Hurricane Ike and Hurricane Harvey. Texans showed their strength during these disasters, and it's certain that the state's residents will continue to make history.

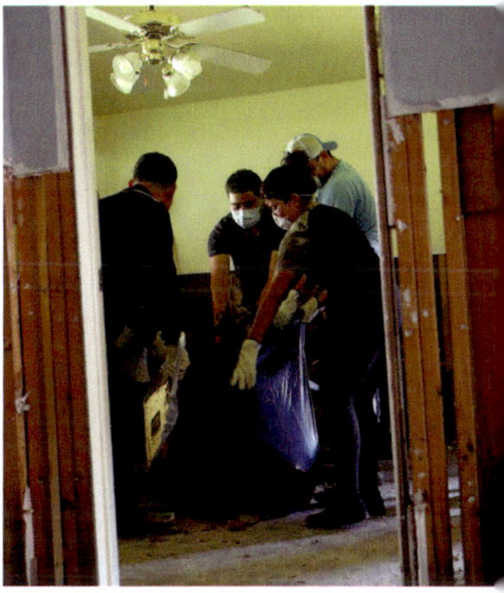

A family starts to clean up after Hurricane Harvey struck their Houston home.

Texans enjoy a festival in downtown Austin.

# 3 Who Lives in Texas?

Texas is a place of great diversity. A common Texas saying goes, "I may not have been born here, but I got here as fast as I could." It's not just a saying, though. Much of Texas's booming growth comes from people who move from all over the world to work and live there.

Native Americans, Mexicans, and people of African descent have populated the state for hundreds of years. Since the founding of the United States, many **immigrant** populations turned their eyes westward and made their home in Texas too. Even with this diverse population, Texas is still known for one group in particular: cowboys.

## Cowboys

From the Dallas Cowboys of the National Football League to the 55-foot "Big Tex" statue at the state fairground, Texans love cowboys. The modern cowboy no longer has gunfights in the middle of a dusty Texas street or rides along the cattle trails. He or she might be a cattle rancher with a college degree in livestock management. He or she might be a professional rodeo performer or an accountant or a computer

### FAST FACT

The Houston Comets were the only team in history to win four back-to-back Women's National Basketball Association (WNBA) championships. The team was led by the "Big Three": Cynthia Cooper, Sheryl Swoopes, and Tina Thompson. The Comets played in Houston from 1997 to 2008.

programmer who likes to wear western boots and ten-gallon hats. The legend of the tough-as-nails wrangler who lived by the code of the West is part of Texans' heritage.

The biggest cowboy in Texas, Big Tex, is a crowd-pleasing favorite at the Texas State Fair.

## Hispanic Texans

According to US Census Bureau estimates, in 2017 more than one-third of Texans (39 percent) were of **Hispanic** origin. People of Mexican descent make up the largest Hispanic group in the state. Most live in the south, near the Mexican border. Some of these people live in poor neighborhoods called barrios or colonias.

Good jobs are not easy to find in the barrio. Sooner or later, many people who live there end up working in the fields. Each year, migrant farm workers go from farm to farm, following the harvest northward as far as Minnesota. The work is hard, and the wages are low. However, Hispanic Texans are proud of their culture and have a lot to celebrate. Hispanic Texans have made huge contributions to the state's history and culture.

Selena Quintanilla-Pérez's popularity as a Tejano singer led to recognition throughout the music world.

Mexican Americans in Texas have even created their own subculture. It is a blend of Mexico and Texas, known as Tejano (Tay-HAN-oh). The word, like the people it describes, is a blend of "Texan" and "Mexicano." Outside the Mexican American community, Tejano culture is best known for its music.

## African Americans in Texas

The first African Americans in Texas were enslaved. After the Civil War, they struggled to make a place for themselves as free people in a

# A Recipe for Prickly Pear Jelly

## Ingredients

- 27 prickly pears (cactus fruit)
- ¼ cup lemon juice
- 1.75 ounces fruit pectin
- 4½ cups sugar

## Directions

1. Get an adult to help you boil and clean three pint-sized jars and their lids.
2. Peel the prickly pear fruit.
3. Put the fruit in a blender and blend it until it is liquid.
4. Put three cups of the blended fruit in a pot with lemon juice and pectin.
5. Ask an adult to stir the mixture constantly until it comes to a boil.
6. Add the sugar and continue stirring. Keep the mixture at a boil for three minutes.
7. Pour the mixture into your jars, leaving ¼ inch (0.6 cm) at the top. Wipe the rims and screw on lids.
8. Place a rack at the bottom of a large pot and fill the pot halfway with water.
9. Get help bringing water to a boil and carefully lowering the jars in. The water level should be 1 inch (2.5 cm) above the jars.
10. Cover the pot for 15 minutes.
11. Ask an adult to remove the jars. Let them cool for twenty-four hours, then enjoy!

Until the civil rights movement, African Americans and other minorities had to go to separate schools and use separate facilities, like this theater in Waco.

free society. Some moved west and found work as cowboys. Others became sharecroppers—where a person farms a piece of land and is paid with a share of the crop. Most landlords took advantage of black workers and created a system that kept the sharecroppers in poverty. Black people who tried to find employment in other areas were paid less than whites that held the same jobs.

This unequal system affected every area of life. Segregation, and what were known as black codes, kept black people separated from white society. Black people were required to go to separate schools from whites and to use separate facilities, such as restrooms, water fountains, and waiting rooms. In all cases, facilities used by blacks weren't as good as those used by whites. In the schools for African American children, for example, students were taught with outdated textbooks. They had to use old, often broken, lab and playground equipment. Tejanos faced similar discrimination. It was not until the civil rights movement of the 1950s and 1960s that African Americans began to see improvements in their lives.

In the 1900s, Texas had a population shift. People began leaving farms and rural towns for cities. Large numbers of African Americans joined in this move. Today, nearly 40 percent of black Texans live in the urban areas of Dallas and Houston.

Native Americans in Texas celebrate their cultures by attending powwows.

## Native Americans

Dozens of Native American groups once made Texas their home. Today, there are only three federally recognized nations in the state: the Kickapoo Traditional Tribe of Texas, the Alabama-Coushatta Tribe of Texas, and the Ysleta del Sur Pueblo.

The Alabama and Coushatta were both members of the Creek Confederacy, and they spoke Muskogean languages. They share a **reservation** in the Big Thicket region in southeast Texas. Sam Houston originally gave the land to them as thanks for their generosity in caring for settlers who passed through their villages. (Houston had once been a member of the Cherokee tribe in Tennessee and did not support displacing Native people.)

The Tigua of Ysleta del Sur Pueblo in El Paso County are the last Pueblo people in Texas. *Pueblo* is the Spanish word for "town."

# Celebrities from Texas

Beyoncé

Selena Gomez

## Beyoncé

Texas native Beyoncé started her career in Houston as part of a group called Destiny's Child. Later, she launched a solo career that brought her new levels of fame. Beyoncé is the most-nominated woman in Grammy history. In addition to recording music and touring, she is a successful businesswoman.

## Jennifer Garner

Actress Jennifer Garner was born in Houston in 1972. Garner was described in *Rolling Stone* magazine as "a radiant actress of rare spirit and sensitivity." She is also an activist and artist ambassador for Save the Children, advocating for literacy, nutrition, and education.

## Selena Gomez

Selena Gomez was born in Grand Prairie in 1992. Gomez first gained recognition as a child actress. She has performed in several television shows and movies while also focusing on her music career. In 2016, she won the American Music Award for Favorite Pop/Rock Female Artist. Gomez is known for giving back and works with many charities.

## Nick Jonas

Nick Jonas was born in Dallas in 1992. Jonas entered the spotlight as a member of the Jonas Brothers. After the music group disbanded in 2013, Jonas focused on his solo career. In addition to music, Jonas appears in television shows and movies.

## Matthew McConaughey

Actor Matthew McConaughey was born in Uvalde, Texas. He has won dozens of awards for his work in television shows and movies. McConaughey has acted in films of all kinds, from romantic comedies to dramas. He has also lent his voice to characters in animated films such as *Kubo and the Two Strings*. McConaughey and his family live in Austin.

## Willie Nelson

Willie Nelson has become a Texas music icon. The country music star was born in Abbott and currently lives on Luck Ranch in Spicewood. Nelson has been nominated for forty-nine Grammy Awards and has won eight of the awards. Now well into his eighties, Nelson still keeps a busy tour schedule.

Willie Nelson

# Texas Biggest Colleges and Universities

(Enrollment numbers are from *US News and World Report* 2019 college rankings.)

Texas A&M University

Texas State University

Texas Tech University

**1. Texas A&M University, College Station**

(53,065 undergraduate students)

**2. University of Texas at Austin**

(40,492 undergraduate students)

**3. University of Houston**

(37,215 undergraduate students)

**4. Texas State University, San Marcos**

(34,180 undergraduate students)

**5. University of Texas at Arlington**

(33,307 undergraduate students)

**6. University of North Texas, Denton**

(31,405 undergraduate students)

**7. Texas Tech University, Lubbock**

(30,737 undergraduate students)

**8. University of Texas at San Antonio**

(26,444 undergraduate students)

**9. University of Texas Rio Grande Valley, Edinburg**

(24,634 undergraduate students)

**10. University of Texas at El Paso**

(21,341 undergraduate students)

The Texas Tiguas originally came from a pueblo in New Mexico, which was already well established when the Spanish first visited it in 1539. Although the Tiguas have lived in West Texas since the 1670s, they were not officially called a Native American nation until 1968. Ysleta del Sur Pueblo is the oldest community in the state of Texas, and the Tigua Tribal Council is the oldest government in the state.

Many Native Americans are no longer able to live their people's traditional way of life. The Kickapoo once lived in the central Great Lakes region. As a result of conflicts with European settlers, they migrated to Kansas, Oklahoma, and Texas. Although the Kickapoo have a reservation in southeast Texas, they have a sort of dual citizenship with Mexico. They are allowed to move back and forth across the border to live or work.

Many of these groups have found ways to keep their culture alive through museums, education programs, and powwows. At a powwow, Native peoples gather to share traditional foods and crafts and to take part in ceremonies that have been passed down from generation to generation.

The Ysleta del Sur Pueblo are one of three federally recognized tribes in Texas.

## Texans from Around the World

In the 1800s, many European immigrants settled in Texas. Today, some of their descendants enjoy keeping their traditions alive. For example, there is a German singing society in San Antonio and an Italian American cultural society in El Paso. Every year, the Irish music festival draws big crowds to the state fairground in Dallas.

People of Vietnamese descent are among the newest Texans. After the Vietnam War

**FAST FACT**

Houston is the site of the first domed stadium, called the Astrodome. It was considered a modern marvel in 1965 when it was built. However, all the grass on the field died. Artificial grass, also known as "AstroTurf" was developed for the 1966 season.

# The Population of Texas Over Time

Before Stephen F. Austin founded the modern state of Texas, the population of that territory was tiny. Ever since Austin's first successful settlement, however, Texas's population has been on the rise.

The Spanish census in 1792 reported a population of roughly 3,000 inhabitants, mostly people of color. Austin made an effort to grow the population between 1821 and 1835. According to the Texas State Historical Association, there were "5,000 blacks, 30,000 Anglo-Americans, 3,470 Hispanics, and 14,200 Indians in Texas" by 1836, totaling 52,670 residents. In 1845, the last year of the independent Republic of Texas, a tally of votes for the last president shows a population of roughly 125,000.

Texas has always had a diverse population. Today, more than half of all Texans identify as Hispanic, African American, or Asian.

In 1850, the first US census found the population of Texas to be over 200,000. The majority of the population were of European descent. Of the roughly 58,500 African Americans in Texas at that time, more than 58,000 of them were enslaved.

Rapid growth continued. By 1900, Texas was the sixth most populous state in the United States, with a population of 3,048,710. In 1955, Texas still ranked sixth in population, but it had grown to 8,657,000 citizens.

In the 1970s, the majority of Texas's population growth was from immigration from other states. This changed in the 1980s, when the rising population was the result of people moving from other nations. In fact, 76 percent of population growth was from immigration from other countries. By 1980, the Texas population had risen to 14,229,191. Between 1980 and 1990, minority populations grew significantly in Texas. The Hispanic population increased by 45 percent and the black population by 17 percent.

Today, the population in Texas is 28,304,596—the second largest in the nation. The population is also increasingly diverse. Around 42 percent of the population identifies as non-Hispanic white, 39 percent identifies as Hispanic, 13 percent identifies as African American, and 5 percent identifies as Asian.

ended in 1975, many Vietnamese refugees came to the United States. More than fifty-two thousand immigrants from Vietnam chose to settle in Texas. They set up communities in cities such as Dallas, Houston, and Austin, and along the Gulf Coast.

Today, the majority of immigrants who settle in Texas come from Mexico, India, El Salvador, Vietnam, and China.

**FAST FACT**

According to the American Immigration Council, more than one in three immigrants in Texas are US citizens. The council says that more than one-fifth of Texas workers are immigrants. Immigrants are a big part of Texas's economy.

## Immigration and Documentation

Each year, thousands of undocumented immigrants come to Texas and other southwestern states. These are people who do not have the required documents from the US government allowing them to live permanently in the United States. They come mostly from Mexico, though many travel through Mexico from Central and South America. Most are desperately poor people who come seeking work. Others are seeking **asylum**, or safety, from violence.

In 2018, more than sixty thousand people came to the United States through Texas's southern border to seek asylum and escape violence in their countries.

Trying to enter the United States without a passport or other legal papers is dangerous. Some people try to walk across the border in remote desert areas to avoid being caught by US Border Patrol agents. There is a great deal of controversy about these people. Some are outraged that schools and other government services are being used by people who are not legal residents of the United States. They also feel that undocumented immigrants take jobs from legal residents. Others argue that their labor is a good thing and contributes to the US economy.

Many immigrants pay smugglers to help them cross the border. Some of these smugglers simply steal the money without doing what they've promised. Others may transport people in unsafe, cruel conditions. In one case, Border Patrol officers heard pounding from inside a truck and found 113 people crammed together inside. In other cases, people have died from the heat and shortage of air inside the trucks sneaking them over the border.

The United States government is working to encourage people who want to move to the United States to go through the legal process for entering the country. The US Department of Homeland Security has increased patrols and built hundreds of miles of new fencing along the border to prevent people from simply walking in. Law enforcement officials are punishing smugglers and employers who knowingly hire undocumented workers, which is against federal law. State and local governments are trying to deal with the money issues, while social welfare agencies deal with the human ones, such as poverty and abuse.

It's difficult to measure the exact number of people coming across the Mexican border illegally because it is done in secret. However, based on the number of times people were apprehended (caught), it seems like illegal immigration is decreasing. In 2000 there were 1.64 million apprehensions, and by 2017 there were about 300,000.

## Looking to the Future

Many Texans are immigrants. In fact, nearly 17 percent of Texans were born in another country. With such a large immigrant population, Texas must consider many factors as lawmakers decide how to treat the challenging issue of undocumented immigration. New laws would impact not just people seeking asylum in Texas but many of the people who already live there.

Texas's economy is a mix of traditional and cutting-edge industries.

# 4 At Work in Texas

Though it's known for oil fields and cattle ranches, Texas has a lot more to offer the modern economy. Today, in addition to its natural resources, Texas is known for its tech industry and manufacturing. Because of the state's growing population, one of the biggest industries in Texas is real estate (the buying and selling of houses). After all, new Texas residents need a place to live. Texas has continued to be a major provider of energy. In the past, it produced oil and natural gas. In 2017, it provided more wind energy from any other state in the US. The many industries in Texas mean the state has a large and powerful workforce.

***FAST FACT***

Texas's cattle population is estimated to be near twelve million. That's one cow for every two people in the state. Texas has the most cattle of any state in the nation.

## Agriculture

One in seven jobs in Texas is in agriculture. The state produces a variety of agricultural products. Each year, income from these products equals about $20 billion. Half of this comes from beef, as the state leads the nation in raising cattle. Cotton is the number-one field crop, followed by corn,

The Lone Star State accounts for nearly 50 percent of cotton grown in the United States.

sorghum grain, and wheat. Many of the top crops are grown as feed for the cattle industry.

Other agricultural products include milk, chickens, eggs, potatoes, rice, and watermelons. Texas ranks among the five states that grow the most tree crops, such as grapefruits, oranges, and pecans.

## Mining and Mineral Extraction

Spindletop is the gusher that started Texas's oil boom.

On January 10, 1901, a domed hill in southeastern Texas made history. Oil drillers had been working at Spindletop for weeks, with no results. That January morning did not begin well. Mud oozed up from the ground, filling the hole and getting in the way of the drill pipe.

Geologist Pete Nester explains what happened next: "After a short time, the … workers set about to clean up the mess … All of a sudden, a noise like a cannon shot came from the hole, and mud came shooting out of the ground like a rocket. Within a few seconds, natural gas, then oil followed … rising to a height of more than 150 feet. This was more oil than had ever been seen anywhere in the entire world."

That day was the beginning of the oil industry in Texas. Hundreds of wells were drilled in the Spindletop area, and in 1902, 17.5 million barrels of oil were pumped out of the ground. The oil fields at Spindletop helped make the United States, for many years, the world's largest producer of oil. In 2018, the United States again

# 3D Printers: A Texas Invention

While a graduate student at the University of Texas in the 1980s, Carl Deckard began developing the technology for 3D printing. Deckard's first prototype (a sample built for testing) was made with a laser and a scanner. Deckard named this first model "Betsy."

In his early experiments, Deckard had to shake plastic particles into the machine by hand in order to make rough plastic hunks. Though what Deckard was printing wasn't sophisticated, he proved 3D printers could work. His early idea went through many changes over the next thirty years before it became what we think of as 3D printing today.

Today, 3D printing is widely available to print all kinds of objects. People use 3D printers to make everything from auto parts to artwork. This powerful tool has made it possible for other inventors to make inexpensive drafts of their ideas by printing parts that would otherwise be difficult to make by hand or expensive to manufacture.

3D printing was invented by Carl Deckard during his graduate studies at the University of Texas in Austin.

became the world's top oil producer. Texas is the top-producing US state by far. In fact, if Texas were its own country, experts say it would be the third-largest producer of oil in the world.

**FAST FACT**

More wool comes from the state of Texas than any other state in the United States. The wool industry has been a part of Texas since the first Spanish settlers arrived. Texas is especially known for its mohair production. Mohair is the long, silky hair of an angora goat.

## Manufacturing

Manufacturing in Texas started with natural products. Food processing plants, textile (cloth) mills, and oil refineries were the early ones. Then manufactured products such as shoes, cars, and electronics were added.

In the 1990s, factory production decreased in industrial states such as Ohio, Pennsylvania, and New York. In Texas, it grew. By 2012, Texas ranked second only to California in the size of its manufacturing workforce.

## Technology in Texas

"High-tech" is a term that has come to stand for modern information and communication technologies. The entire industry began in Texas on September 12, 1958. On that day, electrical engineer Jack Kilby demonstrated his new invention: the microchip, or "integrated circuit." These tiny devices have made the computer and communications revolution possible.

Kilby worked for what was then a medium-sized electronics company called Texas Instruments (TI). Today, TI is a giant in the field, with more than thirty-five thousand employees worldwide. Jack

In 1958, Jack Kilby changed technology forever when he unveiled his new invention: the microchip.

## Texas Instruments

The word "computer" was originally used to mean "one who does computations," and the word actually referred to people! The meaning of the word changed after calculating machines were invented. The very first handheld computer was called a calculator. These handheld devices may seem like simple technology today, but when they first became available to the public, they represented an enormous leap in technology.

Texas Instruments invented the handheld calculator in 1967. This photo shows one of the company's early calculators.

The handheld calculator was invented by Texas Instruments (TI) in 1967. Based in Dallas, Texas, TI has become one of the most recognizable brands of handheld calculators. You might have seen a TI calculator in your own classroom. TI's graphing calculators are so common in American math classes that the company has sold over seventy-five million of them since 1990.

While Texas may be most famous for cacti and cowboys, Texas Instruments helped pave the way for Texas's big role in new technology. The state's reputation for scientific breakthroughs has been growing.

**FAST FACT**
Many famous snack foods were invented in Texas. Dr. Pepper was invented in Waco in 1885. Frito chips were invented in Texas in 1930, and "stadium nachos" were first concocted in 1976 at a Texas Rangers baseball game when Frank Liberto combined cheese sauce with jalapeno juice and dispensed it from a pump.

Kilby was celebrated as a pioneer of the high-tech industries. In 1982, he became a member of the National Inventors Hall of Fame. In 2000, he was awarded the Nobel Prize for Physics.

The development of the microchip helped to turn Texas into a center of high-tech commerce. In 2013, Texas was the second-ranked state for number of high-tech jobs, and it was ranked fourth for adding jobs in technology.

## Tourism

Texas is one of the most visited states in the nation. Texas makes about as much money from tourism as it does from agriculture or manufacturing. People come to Texas for many reasons. Some like the excitement of the cities. Others prefer relaxing on Gulf Coast beaches. Families might spend a day or two at the Six Flags Over Texas amusement park near Dallas–Fort Worth or tour NASA's Lyndon B. Johnson Space Center.

The state has something for everyone. Texas is home to ninety mountains that reach altitudes (heights) of 1 mile or more. Ten percent

Schlitterbahn Waterparks host two million visitors each year.

of the state is covered with forests, including four national forests and five state forests. Texas also has more than 3,359 miles of shoreline.

Texas also has ten major league teams that bring fans from all over. These teams include the Dallas Cowboys, the San Antonio Spurs, the Houston Rockets, and the Texas Rangers.

Beyond professional sports, Texas offers exciting experiences of all kinds. The state is known for its art museums, including the Houston Museum of Fine Arts and the Dallas Museum of Art. Symphony orchestras perform across the state. Of course, rodeos and line-dances are big draws too.

## Don't Mess with Texas

Texas has a lot to be proud of. The Lone Star State's landscape is special and has to be protected. The state doesn't just protect parks and nature preserves, though. In Texas, taking care of the land is everybody's business. Endangered plants and animals must be protected. Air and water must be kept clean.

Texans work hard to protect their natural resources.

Protecting renewable resources is an important part of the state's environmental program. For example, responsible lumber companies in the state plant as many trees as they cut down. This not only protects the forest habitat but also provides a steady source of timber.

Renewable sources of energy, such as solar and wind power, are also important.

These solar panels are on the roof of a building in Grapevine.

Sunlight and wind are limitless and can be used to produce electricity without polluting the air, water, or land. In 1999, the US Congress passed a law requiring power companies to develop these resources. With its wide-open spaces and sunny skies, Texas can easily use wind and solar power. Right now, photovoltaic (solar) systems are powering everything from school crosswalk signs to people's homes.

In 2017, Texas generated enough wind energy to power over six million homes. It had the highest installed wind capacity of any state: 23,421 megawatts. While the national total for wind energy was 6.3 percent, Texas produced 14.8 percent. Texas continues to build its green energy capacity.

It's not just government programs that protect the environment in Texas. Ordinary citizens also get involved. They recycle, volunteer for community cleanup days, and insulate their houses to use less energy.

## A Changing Economy

Since the 1950s, Texas has become more dependent on modern technology and less dependent on oil. New jobs have been created in technology and science, especially since the 1970s and 1980s with the invention of personal computers. New industries have also helped shape a new Texas economy. These changes have worked hand in hand with a steady population boom. Texas's many advancements keep drawing people from all over the world to the Lone Star State. Many businesses choose to bring their companies to Texas for the state's large, skilled workforce. With these many changes, where Texas is headed is as exciting as how far it has come.

The Texas state capitol opened in 1888.

# 5 Government

Texas's constitution has been in effect since February 15, 1876. Since then, it's seen more than 450 changes. The constitution was even rewritten seven times.

The state constitution is important because it outlines how Texas's government works. States, like the federal government, have their own set of laws and rules that determine how the state runs and what is expected of its citizens. The state government makes laws that everyone in the state must obey. It also makes policies for education, health care, and social welfare.

The Texas state government has three branches: executive, legislative, and judicial. The governor is the chief executive of the state. The legislature makes its laws, and the courts settle legal disputes and try criminals.

Policies and programs are often decided at the state level. The counties and cities then carry them out. Texas has 254 counties, and each is run by a commissioners' court. Counties provide services such as schools, public hospitals, libraries, jails, and parks. A county sheriff is responsible for law enforcement.

***FAST FACT***

Texas has "plural executives," or additional executive officers (such as the attorney general) who are elected separately from the governor. Plural executives spread power throughout the government, rather than leaving most of the power in the hands of the governor.

Since 1856, this mansion has housed Texas's leaders, including Governor Greg Abbott.

The Texas legislature in session

Judge Eva Martine Guzman is a member of the Supreme Court of Texas, the highest court of appeals for civil cases.

# Branches of Government

## The Executive Branch

The governor, the head of the executive branch, is elected for a four-year term. He or she can call special sessions (meetings) of the legislature, appoint members of boards and commissions, and veto (reject) or approve bills.

## The Legislative Branch

Like the US Congress, the Texas legislature is divided into two houses—a senate and a house of representatives. The senate has 31 members, elected for four-year terms. The house has 150 members, who serve two-year terms. Both houses must approve a bill before it goes to the governor for final action.

## The Judicial Branch

The judicial branch has two levels of courts: criminal and civil. Criminal cases deal with crimes where people may be sent to jail if they are convicted. Civil cases deal with lawsuits, where one party wants money from another party. (The "party" can be a person, group, or company.) Cases are usually heard first in district court. If a party is unhappy with the decision, they can challenge it in a court of appeals. Cases can be challenged up to the Supreme Court of Texas or the Texas Court of Criminal Appeals. These are the highest courts in the state. Each court has nine judges who are elected to six-year terms.

# Understanding Local and National Government

There are more than one thousand city, town, and village governments in Texas. These governments usually have an elected council. In some cities, a mayor is the head of the local government. In others, a professional city manager is hired to do this work.

Texas has two senators in the US Congress in Washington, DC. As of 2019, the Lone Star State had thirty-six members in the US House of Representatives.

## How a Bill Becomes a Law

Citizens in Texas can play an important part in making laws. If a citizen has an idea for a law, he or she can suggest it to representatives in the state legislature. Sometimes voters will collect many signatures from other voters who share their opinions on an idea. Then they present this petition about a proposed law to legislators. Members of the legislature also come up with ideas for new laws.

A proposed law is called a bill. A representative or person on the representative's staff takes the idea and writes a bill. A bill can be introduced either in the house of representatives or in the senate. If the bill starts in the house of representatives, the house leader assigns a committee to review the bill. The members of the committee hold meetings and discuss the bill. They may make many changes. If they agree that the bill should be a law, they present it to the full house of representatives. The entire house then votes on the bill. If it gets a majority vote, it is sent to the state senate. The senate follows the same procedure. A committee considers the bill, and if it is approved by the committee, then the entire senate votes on it.

When both parts of the legislature have approved a bill, it is sent to the governor. If the governor approves, the bill becomes a law.

Lawmakers must work together and compromise to pass bills.

However, if the governor rejects, or vetoes, the bill, the house and senate still have a chance to pass it. They can hold another vote. If the vote wins by a two-thirds majority, the veto is overturned and the bill becomes a law.

In 1997, an important education law was passed. The law was meant to adapt achievement tests for students with disabilities. How this law passed through legislature is an example of how laws are passed in Texas.

The law first came to the house of representatives on February 27, 1997. It was called HB (House Bill) 1800. It was meant to give students in special-education classes a fair chance to show their skills. Most of the testing changes were a matter of common sense. For example, a blind student cannot be expected to take tests that require the student to read or see directions, and a hearing-impaired student cannot be expected to do well on tests that involve listening.

On March 3, a summary of HB 1800 was read before the full house. It was then sent to the House Committee on Public Education for study. The committee went over it point by point, suggesting changes and asking questions. It held public meetings, which any interested citizen could attend.

When the study was completed, the committee sent the bill back to the full house. After more public readings and debate, the house passed HB 1800 and sent it to the senate. There, it went through the same process of readings, reports, and debates. On May 21, the senate passed the bill. On June 17, 1997, the governor signed HB 1800 into law.

By that time, this simple bill had gone through forty-five different actions. If it had been more complicated or more controversial, it might have taken even longer to pass. There is a good reason for all this complexity. Texas,

# Staying Informed

Today, social media makes it easy to stay informed. The official Twitter handle for the Texas Democrats is @texasdemocrats. The official Twitter handle for the Texas Republicans is @TexasGOP. ("GOP" is short for "Grand Old Party," which is another name for the Republican Party.) Following both parties can give you a broad understanding of events and help you understand how people feel on both sides of an issue. (Be sure to always ask a trusted adult before you log on to social media.)

The two major political parties often post about key members of government and their thoughts about new bills and important events in government. Both parties post regularly about the candidates they support, as well as their opinions about current events and elections. You'll also learn about upcoming legislation and public appearances by local, state, and national politicians.

Because these accounts frequently link to the candidates they are referring to, they give followers access to information about those candidates and a way to contact them directly. Never before in history have the people who represent you in government been so easy to reach.

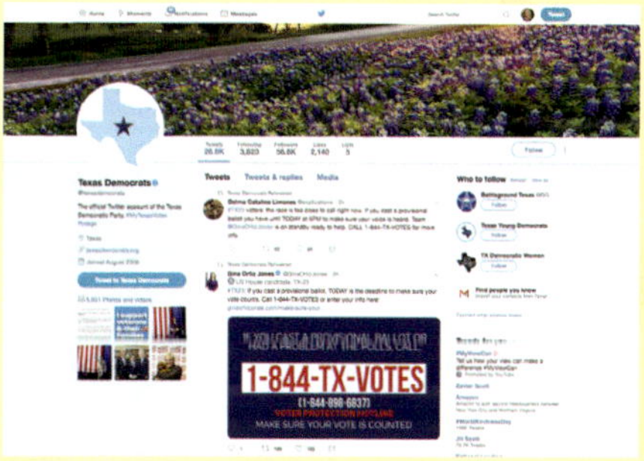


The official Twitter accounts for the Democratic and Republican Parties of Texas are @texasdemocrats and @TexasGOP.

A member of the elections commission staff prepares a polling place for voters in Nacogdoches.

just like other states, wants to be sure that laws are passed fairly. The citizens of Texas need to have a say in their laws. Debate over laws is part of the democratic process.

## A Bright Future

Today, Texas faces many important issues that must be decided on by the people of Texas and the legislature. In addition to immigration and border security, many people are worried about the political process itself. Some Texans worry about voter laws that keep people from voting in elections. Others worry that people might vote when they're not legally allowed to. Like in other US states, Texans also care about education, health care, and public safety.

Democrats and Republicans may not always agree on the best way to address these issues, but they are often key issues for both groups. One thing both parties can agree on is the importance of being prepared for a disaster. Because Texas has seen natural disasters in recent years, many Texans want to know the government has a clear plan in case another hurricane should come. This is especially important as Texas's population grows and more people are affected by events in the state. After all, the politicians and people of Texas know how to work together to move their great state forward.

# Glossary

**asylum** The protection offered by another nation to citizens leaving their country because they are in danger there.

**cattle rustler** Someone who steals cattle.

**climate** The average weather conditions of a particular place or region over a period of years.

**cowboy** A person who tends cattle or horses.

**Hispanic** A person living in the United States who speaks Spanish. A Hispanic person may have been born in a Latin American country like Mexico, or they may have ancestors from a Spanish-speaking country.

**immigrant** A person who comes to a country to live there.

**irrigation** Man-made watering systems.

**manufacturing** Making a product from raw materials, either by hand or using machines.

**Native Americans** People who lived on the North American continent before the arrival of Europeans.

**oil** A thick liquid that comes from wells drilled in the ground and is the source of gasoline, kerosene, and other products.

**polls** Voting places.

**population** The total number of people living in a country or region.

**reservation** An area set aside for use by Native Americans to continue to live by tribal laws and rights.

**secede** To leave a country and become independent.

**settler** A person who moves into and stays in a new region.

**unalienable rights** Rights that can never be taken away.

Rita Blanca National Grassland
Canadian R.
Amarillo
Red R.
Wichita Falls
Lake Texoma
Eisenhower Birthplace State Historic Site
Texarkana
Lubbock
Denton
Plano
Irving
Garland
Fort Worth
Dallas
Arlington
Longview
Tyler
Trinity R.
Guadalupe Peak
Guadalupe Mountain National Park
El Paso
Big Spring
Abilene
Colorado R.
Odessa
Midland
Pecos
San Angelo
Waco
Davy Crockett National Forest
Nacogdoches
Killeen
Brazos R.
Rio Grande
Pecos R.
Bryan
College Station
Sam Houston National Forest
Sabine R.
Austin
Colorado R.
Amistad National Recreation Area
Amistad Reservoir
Big Bend Ranch State Park
Big Bend National Park
Del Rio
New Braunfels
San Marcos
San Antonio
The Alamo
Houston
Pasadena
Beaumont
Sugar Land
Galveston
Victoria
Eagle Pass
Nueces R.
Aransas National Wildlife Refuge
Corpus Christi
Laredo
Gulf of Mexico
Padre Island National Seahore
Falcon Reservoir
Laguna Atascosa National Wildlife Refuge
McAllen
Brownsville
Interstate
Major Highway
City or Town
State Capital
Highest Point in State
Historic Site
National Forest
National Park
State Park
National Wildlife Refuge
Other Points of Interest
N
S
E
W
0
miles

# Texas State Map and Map Skills

## Map Skills

1. What is the northernmost city or town on this map?
2. What is the highest point in Texas?
3. What body of water borders Texas?
4. What is the westernmost city or town in Texas?
5. To get from Lubbock to Big Spring, what direction would you travel?
6. Which historic site is outside San Antonio?
7. What is the southernmost city or town in Texas?
8. To get from Houston to San Marcos, what direction would you travel?
9. What interstate connects Abilene and Fort Worth?
10. Which river runs through Sugar Land?

**Answers:**

1. Amarillo
2. Guadalupe Peak
3. Gulf of Mexico
4. El Paso
5. South
6. The Alamo
7. Brownsville
8. West
9. I-20
10. Brazos River

# More Information

## Books

Gibson, Karen Bush. *Texas History for Kids: Lone Star Lives and Legends.* Chicago: Chicago Review Press, 2015.

Hale, Nathan. *Nathan Hale's Hazardous Tales: Alamo All-Stars.* New York: Amulet Books, 2016.

Parker, Mary O., and Jeff Parker. *Explore Texas: A Nature Travel Guide.* College Station, TX: Texas A&M University Press, 2016.

Rodgers, Kelly. *The Texas Revolution: Fighting for Independence.* Huntington Beach, CA: Teacher Created Materials, 2012.

## Websites

**Kids' House**
https://kids.house.texas.gov/cowpokes/index.htm
The Texas House of Representatives hosts this site filled with activities, links, and information about the politicians in the Texas house.

**Texas Parks and Wildlife Kids**
https://tpwd.texas.gov/kids
Browse special events, find information about the Junior Ranger program, and more on the official website for Texas Parks and Wildlife.

**Texas Senate Kids**
https://senate.texas.gov/kids/kids.htm
Take a virtual tour of the Texas state capitol, read state trivia, and learn more about Texas state senators.

# Index

Page numbers in **boldface** refer to images. Entries in **boldface** are glossary terms.